T0196542

Music Education in Crisis:

Practical Strategies in an Era of Budget Cuts

By Joseph T. Pergola
George Ober

authorHOUSE®

AuthorHouse™
1663 Liberty Drive
Bloomington, IN 47403
www.authorhouse.com
Phone: 1-800-839-8640

Published by AuthorHouse   05/23/2012

ISBN: 978-1-4772-0312-5 (sc)
ISBN: 978-1-4772-0311-8 (e)

Library of Congress Control Number: 2012907943

Any people depicted in stock imagery provided by Thinkstock are models, and such images are being used for illustrative purposes only.
Certain stock imagery © Thinkstock.

This book is printed on acid-free paper.

Because of the dynamic nature of the Internet, any web addresses or links contained in this book may have changed since publication and may no longer be valid. The views expressed in this work are solely those of the author and do not necessarily reflect the views of the publisher, and the publisher hereby disclaims any responsibility for them.

Limits of Liability and Disclaimer of Warrantee:

The author and publisher of this book have used their best efforts in preparing the book and the programs contained in it. These efforts include the development, research, and testing of the theories and programs to determine their effectiveness. The authors and publishers make no warrantee of any kind, expressed or implied, with regard to these programs or the documentation contained in this book.

The authors and publishers shall not be liable in the event of incidental or consequential damages in connection with, or arising out of, the furnishing, performance or use of the programs, associated instructions and/or claims of productivity gains.

Notice:
Music Education in Crisis: Practical Strategies in an Era of Budget Cuts logo is a trademark of the National Education Service Company.
Music Education in Crisis: Practical Strategies in an Era of Budget Cuts logo for commercial purpose without prior written consent of N.E.S.C.O. may constitute trademark infringement in violation of Federal and State laws.

Dedication

To Richard J. Hawkins for his exemplary leadership as a music director and a district superintendent. His support for music education inspired us and revealed a unique understanding of the important role music plays in the education of the whole child. His efforts to build support for music education were a valuable contribution and example for all educators.

Table of Contents

"Math and science are not the opposite of art and music. They are compatible to a well rounded education."
President Barack Obama

"Dumbest mistake we have made in education in this country in the last generation is cutting music and art programs out of our education system."
Governor Mike Huckabee

"A financial crisis always exposes the underlying educational philosophy of a school district."
Dr. John Benham

"Our schools tend to refine intellects but neglect to discipline emotions. For anyone to grow up complete, music is important."
Paul Harvey

Chapter 1

The Crisis

These are trying times for music educators across the nation. The nation is in the grip of a severe recession or depression. Our state and local governments are suffering from severe financial shortfalls which have resulted in severe budget cuts. The brunt of these budget cuts are falling on public service institutions particularly our public schools. In some cases funding cuts are endangering the very existence of music education programs in our schools.

What Happened!
We are in the worst financial crisis since the Great Depression, precipitated by a collapse of major financial institutions, a sharp decline in credit availability and a plunge in the stock market. This national crisis has sunk the country into a long and deep recession. Wide scale job losses creating record high unemployment and the collapse of the housing market causing a loss of home equity, numerous foreclosures and prolonged vacancies are the result. This major decline in consumer wealth has generated less consumer spending and less business

investment producing less taxes.

Such enormous tax shortfalls from revenue reduction from less taxes has made it impossible for local governments to meet their financial obligations.

The largest source of funding for public schools comes from property taxes. The majority of property taxes are levied on home owners.In the current recession where people find themselves in financial crisis, people are not buying homes, not maintaining their homes and, in too many cases, losing their homes to foreclosure. In this type of fiscal environment, state and local governments do not collect the revenue necessary to properly fund local public schools.

The unfortunate reality is this:
with the economy in recession, job losses mounting and severe government budgetary cuts, state and federal money to schools continues to decrease. Yet the cost of operating schools continues to rise. Consider the cost associated with maintaining school buildings. Supplies and services continue to rise in price. The cost of oil alone to heat a school has already risen 20% and is predicted to continue to increase an additional 20% resulting in a 40% overall increase.

The state and the federal government continue to increase educational mandates that are unfunded. These unfunded mandates add greater and greater cost to school budgets.

Most salaries and benefits for school personnel are negotiated a year or more in advance. These salaries and benefits increase over time reflecting the continuing rise in the cost of living. This process of negotiation makes salaries and benefits contractual mandates resulting in fixed costs to the school district regardless of the current fiscal situation.

Sample Average State Budget Deficit Figures
2011-2012

Alabama	$979 million	13.4%
Arizona	$1.5 billion	17.0%
California	$23.0 billion	27.2%
Connecticut	$2.9 billion	14.7%
Florida	$3.7 billion	11.5%
Georgia	$1.3 billion	7.6%
Louisiana	$1.6 billion	19.4%
New Jersey	$10.5 billion	36.0%
New York	$10.0 billion	17.6%
Ohio	$3.0 billion	11.1%
Oklahoma	$500 million	9.0%
Oregon	$1.7 billion	25.5%
Pennsylvania	$3.7 billion	13.4%

* See Appendix for Complete State Deficit Figures

"We never know the worth of water until the well is dry."

Thomas Fuller

Chapter 2

Sad but True

If a school does not recognize the value of music education, the risk of music suffering serious budget cuts is heightened. Too often school leaders and parents lack a true understanding of the importance of music education in a child's development. Music education provides private and public benefits.

Private Benefits:
- Enriches the quality of children's lives
- Promotes cultural awareness.
- Helps students see the world from varying perspectives
- Creates social bonds
- Makes schools better places to learn
- Promotes pride of accomplishment

Public Benefits:
- Promotes responsibility
- Raises student achievement
- Develops self-discipline
- Develops greater tolerance
- Provides constructive entertainment
- Provides pleasure

Throughout the history of education in the United States, the arts have always been vulnerable to cut backs in funding. In the current state of economic recession, public schools lose a significant portion of their funding. This forces school districts to make serious choices about program funding. A loss in funding too often translates into less money to support elective courses in music and art for all students. A significant decrease in fiscal resources can also trigger increased class size and decreased exposure to new technology. Program cuts of this nature are usually accompanied by lay-offs and job cuts.

Unfortunately, the success or failure of a particular music or art department and its students has no direct impact or influence on whether a school receives its fair share of state and federal money. Therefore, school district leaders will continue to focus on academic core classes that require statewide standardized testing.

Numerous studies clearly show that schools with a lower medium household income tend to perform poorer on standardized tests. This most often triggers costly mandated academic intervention services which leave fewer fiscal resources for arts programs.

Schools struggling with academic achievement and showing poor student performance on standardized tests are forced to allocate more and more of their limited resources on core academic subjects. This leaves less and less funding to support encore subjects such as music and art.

Schools with good academic achievement on standardized tests can better afford to allocate resources to subjects such as music and art for the purpose of providing a full well rounded education.

It's sad but true that students attending wealthier school districts have a greater opportunity for a well rounded balanced education that includes comprehensive education in the arts than lower income school districts.

Recent legislation such as "No Child Left Behind" and "Race to the Top" have negatively affected arts education in American schools. "No Child Left Behind" with its obsessive focus on testing in reading and math has disqualified some students from participation in elective art programs and has left little time in an already overcrowded school day for music and art.

According to The National Assessment of Educational Programs in the Arts, student exposure to arts education in schools has steadily declined since 1997.* What makes this decline in student exposure to arts education doubly damaging is the elimination of so many music programs and the decline in the scope of existing programs. It is not uncommon today to see the elimination of elementary instrumental programs, district wide string orchestra programs, grade level choruses and theory classes. Too few schools have maintained specialized co-curricula and advanced placement music courses. Jazz bands, chamber ensembles, recorder groups and keyboard classes have all been relegated to the world of extra-curricular activities.

Public Response:

The state of the economy has created a loss of confidence in government leadership and loss of confidence in the public institutions such as public schools that use the community funds.

Public outrage over ever increasing property taxes has heightened public scrutiny of school budgets. Taxpayers can no longer pay for ever increasing property taxes. The public perception of what is essential for a child's education is narrowing. Everything, except core academic subjects, is starting to be considered a perk.

People are questioning how funds are allocated, the salary and benefits paid to staff and administrators and the expenditures for specific programs.

Recent news reports indicate that virtually every state in the country has had to eliminate teachers.

In spite of all this concern and outrage over increasing taxes and proposed program cuts, public response has not resulted in unified action. We as educators have miscalculated public response. There has been no universal public outcry or demand for action that truly puts children first. We must not mistake concern and sympathy for advocacy.

Result:
Whenever school budgets need to be cut, music programs and music teachers are the first to go! School leaders feel pressured to appease the public with budget cuts and the appearance of fiscal restraint.

Unfortunately, music education continues to remain very low as a national educational priority. State tests exist in most core academic subjects. These tests indicate what is most valued in education and they dictate what schools teach. If a state assesses a particular subject, schools find ways to teach that skill and content or risk the negative consequences of their students not demonstrating mastery.

Question:
Why is it so difficult for so many individuals in decision-making positions to understand the importance of maintaining a strong music program?

The answer is simple! We must face the fact that we collectively and as individuals, have not done a good enough job communicating the value of music education for our children's future and for our nation. We have not effectively communicated and convinced the academic world, society in general, the people who control the levers of influence and the people who make the critical decisions regarding educational funding for the arts.

It is estimated that a majority of Fine Arts Departments in public schools have adopted funding and/or program cuts for 2011-2012 (and look to cut further in 2012-13)

In the past six decades, music education in public schools has suffered numerous threats to its funding and in some cases to its very existence.

- In the 1950's we saw a huge shift in available funds to science as a response to the early Soviet success in space.
- The social upheaval of the 1960's and the Civil Rights movement required new funding for curriculum revision and a focus on the social sciences.
- The recession of the 1970's followed by massive inflation shrunk the value of the dollar and threatened all school budgets.
- The 1980's saw a shrink in public school populations resulting in tax shortfalls.
- The TaxPac movement of the 90's resulted in a large number of failed school budgets resulting in wide-spread austerity funding.

Despite six decades of education funding problems, one would expect that public school advocates would have developed numerous procedures and strategies that have been formulated and tested for effectively dealing with a funding crisis.

"Upon the subject of education, I can only say that I view it as the most important subject which we as a people may be engaged in."

-Abraham Lincoln

Chapter 3

Lessons from the Past

Unfortunately, the facts show that we have learned little from past problems. Although educational music associations have unveiled broad based advocacy plans, most are nothing more than glorified public relations programs placed in the hands of an organized leadership as opposed to inspired grass-roots movements emphasizing prevention.

The development and implementation of state and national standards for music education have accomplished little to secure a place for music as a core subject in public schools.

Music educators must learn to be proactive. Too often we don't see the threat to music education coming until it's to late!

Too many school boards believe that cutting or eliminating music programs will ease budget restraints with little or no detrimental effect on students. It is the responsibility of every music education advocate to be able to effectively dispute this claim.

We must learn how to collect and analyze critical data in order to effectively use that data to support our case. Accurate data can show the negative impact of program cuts on a proposed budget.
Data that measures student enrollment in each aspect of the music program and the ratio of staff to students will reveal the true value and cost of that program.

Whenever program or funding cuts are made to music programs, school boards always claim that the arts are not being unfairly targeted. They will site cuts to other programs beside music. But the truth is that cut backs in the arts have never been proportionately fair when compared to cut backs in other programs.

When an elementary or feeder program such as beginner band, orchestra or chorus is eliminated, extensive national case studies show a 65% minimum decline in student participation at the secondary level.

If a school with one thousand students proposes cuts equalling one teacher in each subject area, they can easily make the case for fairness. But in reality, cutting one math teacher when every student must take math means one of eight math teachers will be eliminated or 12.5% of math staff.*

But one music teacher in a typical school with a band, orchestra, chorus and classroom music teacher results in one of five music teachers eliminated or 20% of the staff.

I ask, is that fairness?

*(based on 5 period teacher load of 5 teaching periods per day@ 25 students per class)

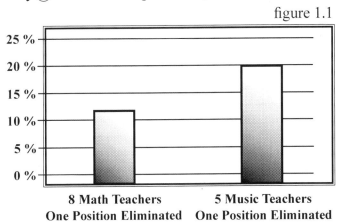

figure 1.1

8 Math Teachers
One Position Eliminated

5 Music Teachers
One Position Eliminated

(*John Benham - Focus on Budget: Reverse Economics)

A school district with 400 middle school instrumental students; 210 in band and 180 in orchestra taught by 1 band director and 1 orchestra director, decides to eliminate 6th grade band with an enrollment of 70 students and 6th grade orchestra with a total enrollment of 60 students. This loss of 130 students from the middle school program will result in the necessity to create a minimum of 5 new classes if class size is limited to 26 students. That's the equivalent cost of 1 new full time academic teacher while still maintaining the current band and orchestra staff in order to provide music instruction for the 270 of the original 400 students remaining in the 7th and 8th grade instrumental program.

This proposed cost saving in reality results in the hiring of additional staff or paying to cover the classroom placement of students no longer participating in music performance groups.

(*John Benham - Focus on Budget: Reverse Economics)

Chapter 4
Common Reactions
and
Misguided Steps

The Center for Budget and Policy Priorities reports that at least 46 states are faced with severe fiscal shortfalls. Recent estimates total deficits at more than 48 billion dollars. This figure is expected to widen as economic turmoil continues. As a result 33 states have cut or made proposals to cut music education programs with additional states and additional cuts to follow.
* website - http://www.cbpp.org/

Tactical Mistakes

Mistake #1	Understanding the Problem

Before any action is taken in response to proposed budget or program cuts, it is essential that everyone understand the depth and scope of the problem. Like most fiscal budgetary problems, the true cause of the problem is often complex.

Such complicated problems are rarely the result of a single individual's action. Most often, responsibility is the result of multiple actions by numerous people.

A thorough understanding of the problem will serve as an invaluable guide in the development of an action plan and help in avoiding tactical errors which can make the situation worse rather than better.

Mistake #2	No Target Audience

Complain to everyone, complain often and complain loudly. This often seems to be the approach by educators facing severe budget or program cuts. As musicians, we are all familiar with the adage "preaching to the choir". Complaining to everyone, complaining often and complaining loudly may generate sympathy but it is not likely to generate positive change. Besides having the potential of being an annoyance, constant complaining will also cast you in the light of being selfish and part of the problem instead a source of the solution.

Before we contemplate any action in response to budget or program cuts, it is critical that we identify our target audience.

There are three groups that we must target:
1. State Legislatures that allocate state aid.
2. School Boards that make policy and submit annual budgets.
3. Parents who elect school board members.

All our efforts must be focused on influencing those entities that have the authority to make budgetary decisions.

Mistake #3   Lacking a Strategy

Lacking a comprehensive strategy for combating proposed budget and program cuts is a common mistake. Not designing a strategy makes it near impossible to choose the most effective options in addressing a pending threat to the structure of the program.

Plan for dealing with budget cuts before you are forced to do so!
An effective strategy will examine and critically appraise each of the strategic options available, and determine where and how to direct its effort, before selecting the best solution.

A well developed strategy should be consistent in approach but flexible in the outcome. It should lay out all options and take all factors into account including the school's mission, environment, capabilities and values. A thorough strategy serves as a map designed to guide one from what is proposed to where one desires to end up. Be sure your strategy provides critical data and facts to support your priorities.

Remember, only with a comprehensive strategy can we effectively advance an alternative position. If we are not prepared, we will be the victims of someone else's plan!

Mistake #4 Proposing A Compromise

One of the most common mistakes music education advocates make when faced with proposed budget cuts is to propose compromise cuts that preserve preferred parts of the music program. This relieves the administration and school board of responsibility for cuts and allows them to report to the public that the cuts enacted were suggested by the music teachers.

Remember, Program cuts suggested are likely to be program cuts enacted.

Mistake #5 Compare and Contrast

Avoid becoming involved in a battle of music verses other co-curricular or extra-curricular programs. It is a mistake to engage in such comparison and contrast. Always project an understanding that all programs have value. Diminishing the importance of another program will not build allies for your cause. It will make the music department seem petty, selfish and uncommitted to the school's entire educational vision.

Mistake #6   Unprofessional Behavior

Personal attacks, insults and threats will harm your professional reputation and weaken your cause. No one likes to be insulted or threatened. It breeds revenge and creates enemies. Such behavior will be seen as a desperate strategy and a sign of weakness for your cause. Always take the high road! Stay focused on the issues and defend the best interest of the students. Study the situation, offer your help, and present solutions. Be part of the solution, not part of the problem!

Mistake #7   Scapegoating

Scapegoating and playing the blame game are two of the most damaging and unproductive reactions in which you can engage. Usually created out of frustration, scapegoating and blaming relieve individuals of personal responsibility.

Playing the blame game never works. A deep set of research shows that people who blame others for collective or personal mistakes lose status, earn less, and perform worse relative to those who own up to mistakes. It is common for people to take credit for success while minimizing failure.

Research also shows that the same applies for organizations. Groups and organizations with a rampant culture of blame have a serious disadvantage when it comes to creativity, learning, innovation, and productive risk-taking.

Blaming is contagious! Psychologists tell us that "blame" is a lack of personal responsibility that keeps people stuck in the active throes of suffering.

Scapegoating and blaming is a game that nobody actually has a chance of winning. It's a game that hurts all involved and contributes nothing to an already desperate situation.

In addition to being frustrating and a waste of time, the blame game can also be very counterproductive. By shifting the focus to who made the mistake which led to the problem, the blame game distracts people from why the problem occurred in the first place. As a result, the members of the group may miss out on a valuable learning experience which would have allowed them to prevent such errors in the future.

Mistake #8	Not Involving Parents

One of the biggest mistakes that a growing and successful music program can make is not involving parents in shaping and protecting the vision of the music program. Statistics regarding public support for music education are extremely favorable. Clearly a vast majority of parents believe in the importance of music education and support the existence of performance ensembles in their school district.

Parents are a very powerful voice in school districts. Although often unaware, parents control the levers of power. They elect school board members and pass or fail the school district budget. Parent booster groups that support and advocate for music programs are essential. Mobilizing these supportive parents is the challenge.

Effective communication builds advocacy and effective advocacy mobilizes parent action.

Traditional advocacy vehicles such as community outreach programs and positive public relations in local newspapers and on local radio and TV, are no longer sufficient in the new economic reality shaping public education. We must use every available method and medium to communicate and mobilize parents. Besides traditional newsletters, music departments need to have a strong presence on the District's web site. Every teacher should maintain an online bulletin board. Department heads should prepare talking-points for parent advocacy groups communicating with board of education members and administrative supervisors. Today it is possible to instantly email every music parent on a regular basis. Do you have the email addresses of every music parent? Have you encouraged every music parent to open a Twitter and Facebook account as an additional source for communicating information. Both these social network services provide a too often untapped source for improving communication and motivating advocacy and action.

Mistake #9   Passing the Buck

The act of transferring responsibility for a problem everyone should deal with onto a single individual or select group is called passing the buck.

When faced with big problems, it is not uncommon for individuals to expect someone else to solve their problem. Too often music teachers see themselves in a limited role. It's their job to teach and someone else's job to deal with and solve problems.

This limited vision of the teacher's role is shortsighted and unproductive. Transferring responsibility for a problem on to another is not only a way to evade the work needed to resolve the problem but it conveniently provides an excuse for inaction. The most destructive aspect of evading responsibility is that is provides someone else to blame for the situation and/or the outcome.

The truth is everyone affected by a problem has a responsibility to contribute to the solution of that problem.

Mistake#10   Poor Communication

If professionals don't take the trouble to pass necessary information along to support staff, poor communication is the result.

There are many opportunities for poor communication in a workplace, and awareness of these hindrances is the first step toward discovering and solving them.

The way in which people communicate can actually be the cause of poor communication in the workplace. Even if the person with the necessary information believes that he/she has shared the information with all of the correct people, this may not exactly be true. After all, some people are better at communicating than others, and when someone who struggles to express himself is the source of the necessary information, this causes a problem. It is very important that an effective spokesperson be chosen to communicate all important information.

Not having an appointed spokesperson results in multiple messengers delivering multiple messages. To avoid confusion and create solidarity in message and mission, an articulate supported spokesperson is essential.

Mistake #11   Giving Up

When is a loss a loss? When you give up trying to
avoid or reverse a potential loss. Often when presented
with a serious threat to our music programs, we become
defeatists. After all, what can we do? As teachers we
often feel we are powerless. If the Board of Education,
Superintendent and other District Office administrators
are recommending or endorsing budget or program cuts,
there is little to nothing we can do. It is their job to make
policy. They have all the power. Not true!

Unlike teachers with tenure and job security, Board
of Education members are elected officials. Their job
security depends on the approval of the community.
They can be re-elected or defeated in the next election.
Superintendents and other Central Office administrators
are hired by the Boards of Education. If they embarrass
or jeopardize the standing of Board members in the
community, they run the risk of losing their credibility
and influence, or they may not remain Central Office
Administrators.

School District leadership is a political process and we
better learn to become much more politically savvy and
politicly active.

Never forget! Nothing lasts forever!
This too will change!

Never forget!
Nothing lasts forever!

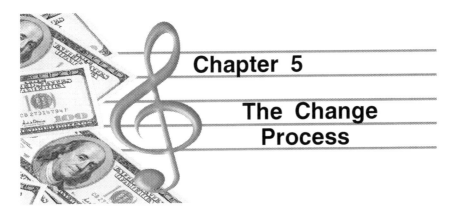

Chapter 5

The Change Process

Crisis is an opportunity to take a fresh look at educational goals, policies and practices and to re-evaluate what is truly important and what truly works. It's an opportunity to re-define the best possible education for our children.

It's hard to deal with change. Change can be very upsetting. However, change is a way of life and systems often change as well. To avoid instability, change needs to be managed and understood before we can expect people to accept it. Change must be realistic and achievable. It cannot be imposed!

First and foremost, everyone must understand that budget cuts aren't being made to spite anyone.

They are due to fiscal issues.

Effective management of change entails:

1. Thoughtful planning
2. Sensitive implementation
3. Consultation

Ask yourself?:

- What do you want to achieve?
- Who is effected?
- How will they react?

A clear vision can help everyone understand why you're asking them to change. When people see for themselves what you're trying to achieve, then the changes recommended tend to make more sense. We must communicate, facilitate and enable involvement from all constituent groups as early and as fully as possible.

Change Management Principles

1. At all times involve the people within the system.

2. Understand the current state of the music program.

3. Understand where you want the music program to be.

4. Plan development toward appropriate and achievable stage

*www.businessballs.com/changemanagement.htm

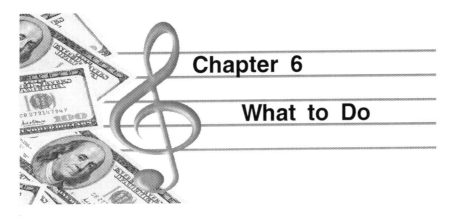

Chapter 6

What to Do

Each music department must develop a set of procedures or guidelines to follow when dealing with a budgetary emergency. Implementing these procedure will allow one to make the best possible decisions based on the best information.

Step 1:   Create a Crisis Management Team

Experienced and knowledgable individuals should compile information necessary to educate the entire staff. This Crisis Management Team will be responsible for compiling up-to-date information for a capable member of the team appointed to serve as department spokesperson.

Step 2: Set a Goal

Maintaining a goal committed to minimize the impact of budget cuts on the music program will help focus your thinking, reveal your options and shape your recommendations.

This process of goal setting helps you recognize what you must do. By knowing precisely what you must do, you know where to concentrate your efforts. Be sure the goal you are working toward is reasonably achievable, not just something that sounds good.

Step 3: Prioritize

Prioritize all sections of the music program regardless of whether or not they are affected by proposed fiscal cuts. These should include bands, orchestras, choruses, classrooms, keyboard labs, theory classes, administrative issues, etc:

Rate each department program on a scale from highest to lowest.

Highest Ratings = Programs most successful for the most number of students and completely supported by district leadership,

Lower Ratings = Programs less successful or serving a small number of students.

Lowest Rating = A program whose value is not worth its' cost.

Step 4: Value Based Budget Analysis

Value Based Budget Analysis is a system of rating each music department program based on the operating cost of the program in relation to its value in meeting or contributing to the music departments priorities. A completed Value Based Budget Analysis will expose every cost factor in your music program and reveal the correlation of cost to value.

figure 1.2

Value Based Budget Analysis Form		
Program	**Cost $**	**Value Ratio (1-?)**

Step 5: Create a Consequence Cost Document

We often take our most successful music programs for granted. The success and value of the programs seems obvious. Too often, education leaders not trained in the arts do not fully understand the true value of a particular music program or its contribution to the students, school and community.

A "Cost Consequence Document" clearly explains the unique importance of a particular music program. It describes the budgetary and educational value of the program, the need to protect the program and the draconian effect of cutting such a program. Your "Cost Consequence Document" should be presented in terms that emphasize the importance of the program to the sequential development of students.

It is imperative that a "Cost Consequence Document" exist for every successful music program to be protected and preserved. Such a document is usually a real "eye opener" for District leadership. It builds respect for in-depth knowledge of the music program and it improves one's level of influence.

Step 6:   Know Your Cost Saving Target

Projected fiscal savings are usually expressed as
individual program or staff cuts. Recommendations to
eliminate staff or programs are made with a specific
cost savings target. Knowing the total amount of money
targeted for savings will allow you to
refocus the conversation from cuts to savings. Knowing
the cost saving target will also allow you to analyze the
recommended cuts and possibly suggest alternative cost
savings.

Step 7:   Develop a Cost Savings Plan

Once a cost savings target has been established, it is time
to map out a Cost Savings Plan to meet the intended
savings target. Your Cost Savings Plan should be based
on the results from your Value Budget Analysis. When
developing your Cost Savings Plan, be sure to include all
aspects of the music program. Examine all instructional
as well as non-instructional costs. No aspect of the
program is exempt from consideration.

Step 8:   Identify Non-Instructional Costs

The first and primary focus of your Cost Savings Plan
should be non-instructional cost. Cut as much non-
instructional costs as possible. Remember, the primary
function of your music program is to provide the best
possible education for the most amount of students.

The music program does not exist for the employment of friends and colleagues. It is shocking how much non-instructional costs can total.

Give special attention to the following items when examining non-instructional costs.

Non-Instructional Student Costs
- Student Travel
- Student Participation Fees
- Student Instrument Costs

Non-Essential Events:
- Awards Nights
- Special Events

Office Supplies:
- Ensemble Folders
- New Music
- Technology
- Copying
- Go Paperless

Administrative Costs:
- Conferences
- Competitions
- Trips
- Professional Development Travel

Auditorium Costs:
- Custodial Costs
- Security Costs
- Chaperone Costs
- Sound and Lighting Crew Costs
- Air and Heat Costs
- ProgramPrinting and Duplication Costs

Step 9. Consolidate and Eliminate Duplication

"More is nice, but not always necessary."
In a fiscal crisis, when severe budget cuts are looming
we must consolidate. The first step in consolidation is
the elimination of duplication. Eliminate duplication of
services wherever possible. Seek to consolidate programs
and services.

Can you combine two different ensembles without
seriously diminishing instructional effectiveness or the
educational value of the program?

Can one teacher do the job of two or can two teachers do
the job of three?

If more teachers are split between buildings, can you
accomplish the same amount and level of instruction?

Does the program need more than one secretary or more
than one coordinator?

Consolidation allows similar programs to unite without
losing the essential service of each program. Think about
how you can become "leaner and meaner".

Step 10:   Institute a Hiring Freeze

Immediately institute a hiring freeze that eliminates the need to replace teachers lost due to budgetary constraints or teachers who retire or resign. Establishing a hiring freeze requires consolidation and dictates the development of a consolidation plan to deal with the elimination of one or more staff positions.

Seek opportunities to use alternative staffing to maintain successful programs without hiring.
• Search for volunteers to teach extra sections.
• Consider running fewer sections of a particular course
• Create additional travel positions to cover more instructional programs.

The benefits of a hiring freeze based on a detailed consolidation plan are immediate savings, employment protection for remaining staff and preservation of programs.

Step 11:   Seek Alternative Funding

Budget shortfalls that do not supply enough funding for particular programs can be supplemented with alternative funding. The best sources of alternative funding are government programs, civic organizations and parents. Consider appointing individuals with connections to each of these organizations as department liaisons. Local, state and national governments provide numerous grants for funding arts education. They also provide corporate support from donors.

Local governments often arrange for sponsorships from various organizations and supporters. These sponsorships can help pay for specific needs such as instrument rentals, theatrical presentations etc.

Civic Organizations are inherently local. Their membership primarily consists of school district residents many of whom are parents of students in the schools. All civic organizations have a commitment to improve their locality. They have fiscal resources and are expert at raising money for causes to which they are committed. Most civic organizations desire to increase their membership. What better way to impress residents than by assisting local schools maintain an effective music program.

No group of individuals has a greater stake in the preservation of the music program than the parents of those students participating in the program. Every school has a PTO or PTA whose sole purpose is to support their school. The main mission of these organizations is to insure proper educational opportunities for all children. Parent groups and individual parents can provide funding, supplies or equipment that can help a music department meet its needs in providing quality music education for students.

When alternative funding sources still do not provide the necessary funds to overcome a budget cut, it is time to consider usage fees and public requests for donations.

Examples:

- Require An Instrument Usage Fee
- Charge Admission at special concerts, festivals, theater productions etc.
- Charge tuition at clinics, camps, summer programs
- Request donations at all audience attended music events

Step 12: Restructure

When everything that can be done has been done and it's not enough it's time to restructure the entire program. Recognize that the music program is not meeting the educational needs of enough students to insure its survival. Do not hesitate! Do not wait any longer! Recommend the replacement or elimination of any failing program that does not meet the instructional or learning goals of the music department. Replace such programs with less costly programs that have a greater chance of success.

Step 13: Advocacy

Design, manage and maintain an ongoing thorough "Advocacy Action Plan". The need for effective professional advocacy is greater now more than ever!

If you believe in what you are doing, "Bang the Drum" and tell people. Remind them of the value of music education. Arm yourself with facts and present your case in a strong but unemotional manner. Solicit supporters such as music booster groups, PTO, donors and influential individuals to help spread the message and speak about the value of music education. The message is important! It must be heard and understood to be

"Are we doing what is best for our students or are we doing what is most convenient for us?"

Anonymous

Chapter 7

The Future

What will your music program look like in the future? Imagine a world without comprehensive music education in our schools! Imagine a program that only provides classroom general music to elementary students! Imagine no instrumental ensembles! Imagine more and more staff members teaching out of their area of specialty! Imagine students having to audition to be selected for the one band, orchestra or chorus in their school! Imagine no pullout lesson program for instrumental students! What does the future hold for music education in our schools? Will formal music education in public schools continue to grow and develop as it has since it began in 1923? Will music education be available to all students in all grades? Will comprehensive music education curricula that are expressive, creative and relevant survive?

Well, the future begins now. Do you want to place the future in the hands of educators who are politicians first and educators second? Do you want to leave the critical decisions about music education to individuals who too often have little or no music education training?

The time to act is now! You can't afford to wait. It takes years to build a quality music program, but it only takes minutes for an uneducated school board and a subservient administration to destroy a quality comprehensive program. Once an education program is lost, it rarely if ever returns. We must remind everyone that the cost of education is far less than the cost of ignorance.

History has taught us that the quantity and quality of music education repeatedly moves through cycles. Prosperous times have been good times for the quantity and quality of music education in public schools. Problematic times have produced difficulties for the quality and quantity of music education. Clearly, we are in a problematic time that is creating great difficulty in the financing of comprehensive music programs. In spite of these difficulties, we must do all we can to insure music education retains its proper place in the school curriculum.

In 1927 and in 1959 the American Association of School Administrators adopted the following statement:

"We believe in a well-balanced school curriculum in which music is included side by side with other important academic subjects."

It is important that pupils, as part of general education, learn to appreciate, to understand, to create and to criticize, with discrimination those products of the mind, the voice, the hand and the body which give dignity to the person and exalt the spirit of man.

Again in 1973 a third statement was adopted by the AASA. It reads, *"As school budgets today come under extreme fiscal pressures, trimming or eliminating so-called peripheral subject areas from the curriculum appears often to be financially attractive. The AASA believes that a well-rounded, well-balanced curriculum is essential to the education of American children. We believe that deleting entire subject areas which have value in the total life experience of the individual is shortsighted. Therefore, AASA recommends that school administrators declare themselves in favor of maintaining a well balanced curriculum at all grade levels, opposing any categorical cuts in the school program."*

It's time to hold school boards and school administrators to their word.

Let's continue to remind them of their own statements.

Education is about developing the whole person and future citizens who can contribute to building a better society. Just as there is more to citizenship than voting and there is more to life than success in business, there is more to education than academic achievement. Music is able to make life more beautiful, profound, enjoyable and interesting.

In spite of music's prominent role in society, we continually have to justify its place in our schools. The future of music education will always be in jeopardy until the education community understands the unique gift of music which is its ability to supply students with valuable experiences that enrich their lives.*

The choice is yours!
"The future belongs to those who prepare for it today."

Malcolm X

Bibliographic References for Leadership Topics

Monday Morning Leadership
By David Cottrell
Corner Stone Leadership Institute
Dalls, Texas

Supervising the Successful School Music Program
By Malcom E. Besson
Parker Publishing, N.Y.

The Art of Teaching
By Gilbert Highet
Vintage Books, N.Y.

"5 Great Leader Traits"
Self Growth Engine.com

"Change Management Steps"
The Center for Secondary School Redsign

School Leadership that Works
By Robert Marzano, Timothy Waters, Brian McNulty
ASCD, Virginia

Why We Need the Arts
American Council for the Arts
N.Y.

Principal Centered Leadership
S.R. Covet
Simon Schuster 1992 N.Y.

The Common Sense Guide to Leadership
By John F. Sullivan
Lincoln, NE

Leadership in a Culture of Change
By Michael Fullan
Jossey-Bass 2001, California

A Fifth Discipline
Schools that Learn
By Peter Senge
Doubleday, NY

Enhancing Professional Practice
S.R. Covey
Simon Schuster 1992 NY

Model Music Programs
M. Blakeslee, L. Brown, A. Hoffman
Rowman and Littlefield, NY

Music Education
Historical Contexts and Perspectives
By Joseph Labutao and Debroah Smith
Prentice Hall, N.J.

Foundations of Music Education
By H. Abedes, C. Huffer, R. Klutman
Schirmer Books, N.Y.

Appendix

Gaps States have Faced in Fiscal Year 2012 in their General Fund Budget

State	Projected Shortfall	Percent of FY2012
Alabama	$979 million	13.4%
Arizona	$1.5 billion	17.0%
California*	$23.0 billion	27.2%
Colorado	$450million	6.2%
Connecticut	$2.9 billion	14.7%
District of Columbia	$322 million	5.1%
Florida	$3.7 billion	11.5%
Georgia	$1.3 billion	7.6%
Hawaii	$540 million	9.8%
Idaho	$92 million	3.6%
Illinois	$5.3 billion	16.0%
Iowa	$149 million	2.4%
Kansas	$492 million	8.1%
Kentucky*	$780 million	8.3%
Louisiana	$1.6 billion	19.4%
Maine	$422 million	13.8%
Maryland	$1.4 billion	9.5%
Massachusetts	$1.8 billion	5.6%
Michigan	$767 million	3.6%

State	Projected Shortfall	Percent of FY2012
Minnesota	$3.8 billion	20.3%
Mississippi	$634 million	13.8%
Missouri	$704 million	8.9%
Nebraska	$166 million	4.8%
Nevada*	$1.2 billion	37.4%
New Hampshire	$250 million	18.4%
New Jersey	$10.5 billion	36.0%
New Mexico	$450 million	8.3%
New York	$10.0 billion	17.6%
North Carolina	$2.4 billion	12.1%
Ohio*	$3.0 billion	11.1%
Oklahoma	$500 million	9.0%
Oregon*	$1.7 billion	25.5%
Pennsylvania	$3.7 billion	13.4%
Rhode Island	$219 million	6.9%
South Carolina	$630 million	11.5%
South Dakota	$127 million	11.0%
Tennessee	DK	Na
Texas	$9.0 billion	20.5%
Utah	$390 million	8.0%
Vermont	$176 million	14.3%
Virginia*	$2.0 billion	12.3%
Washington	$2.5 billion	15.3%
Wisconsin	$1.6 billion	11.5%
States Total	$102.9 billion	15.9%

Value Based Budget Analysis Form		
Program	Cost $	Value Ratio (1-?)

Printed in the United States
By Bookmasters